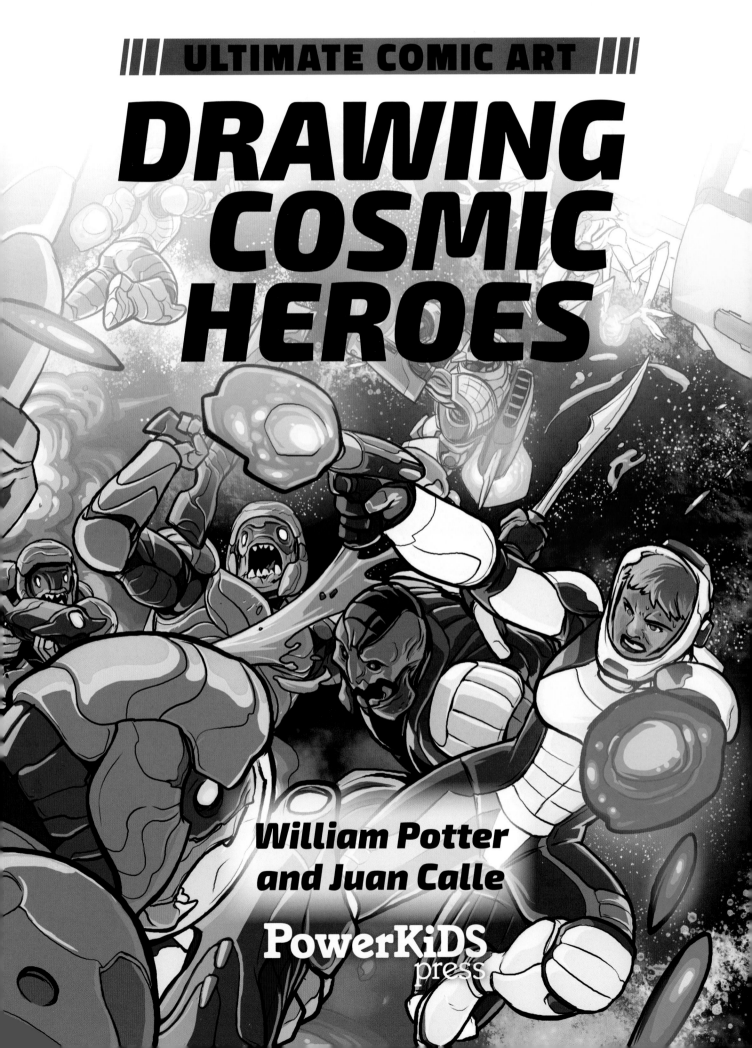

ULTIMATE COMIC ART

DRAWING COSMIC HEROES

**William Potter
and Juan Calle**

PowerKiDS
press

CONTENTS

FROM OUTER SPACE

Outer space is full of wonders to fuel your imagination. Take inspiration from the planets and stars to write your own adventure with cosmic heroes and awesome aliens!

LET'S MAKE COMICS

It's time to create your own comic book story, and this book is full of advice and guides to help you get your ideas onto the page. We'll show you how to create unique characters and locations, and how to draw them in true comic strip style.

STEPS AHEAD

To get your inter-galactic adventure started you'll need a cosmic hero — someone who knows their way around the planets and how to deal with alien foes! Step-by-step instructions will show you how to draw anatomy, and there are guides on drawing action poses and creating scenes from other planets.

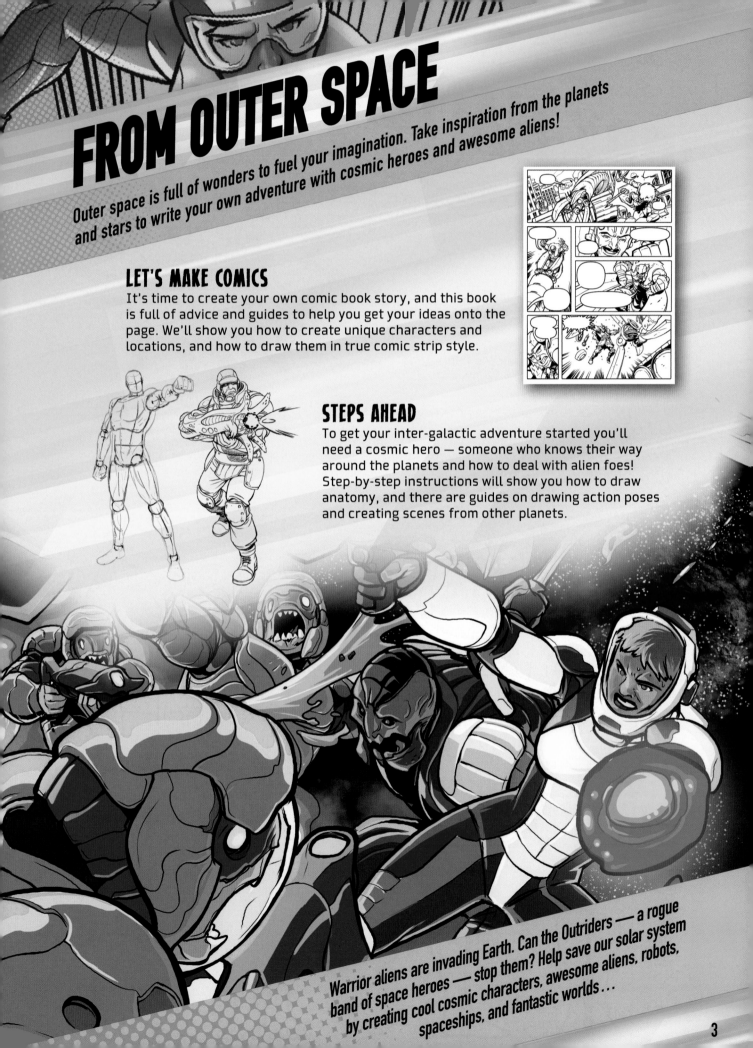

Warrior aliens are invading Earth. Can the Outriders — a rogue band of space heroes — stop them? Help save our solar system by creating cool cosmic characters, awesome aliens, robots, spaceships, and fantastic worlds . . .

BODY MATTERS

When you can draw a figure with accurate proportions, your characters will look more realistic. Superheroes and villains often have exaggerated muscular physiques — some may even have animal or alien features!

The human body is symmetrical, with the bones and muscles on the left matching those on the right.

Men's bodies are often wide at the shoulders and chests, then narrower at the hips. Women's bodies are often narrow at the waist and wider at the hips, like the number 8.

All human bodies are about eight heads tall. The waist is about three heads down from the top of the body, and the hands reach midway down the thigh.

TOP TIP

You don't have to give all of your comic book characters an athletic build. Use different heights and body shapes so that readers find it easier to tell them apart.

When you draw a person standing up straight, you should be able to draw a straight line from the top of their head down through their waist, to their knees, and through the center of their feet. Their shoulders should push out as far as their bottom, while their chest pushes out as far as their toes.

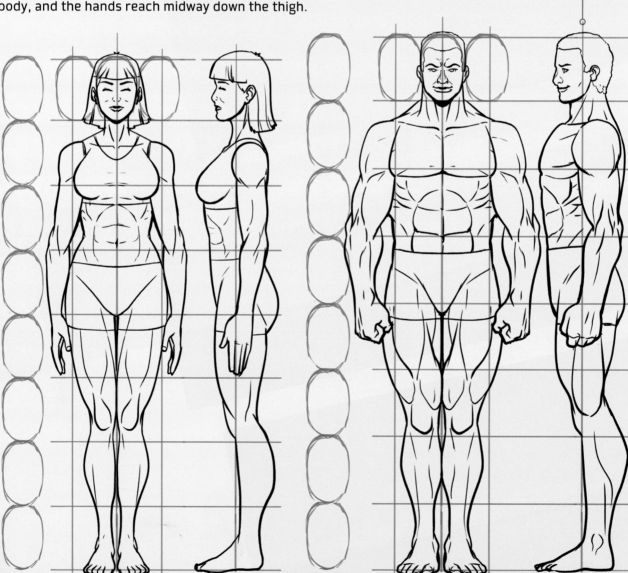

FACE TIME

Faces have their own proportions, with eyes and ears about halfway down the head. Here are average faces you can use for reference.

The ears are about the same height and position as the nose.

The eyes should be one eye-width apart.

Jaws are important to the shape of a person's face. They can be wide and square, narrow and sharp, or round and soft.

The nose forms an imaginary triangle with one point above the nose and one point on either side of the mouth.

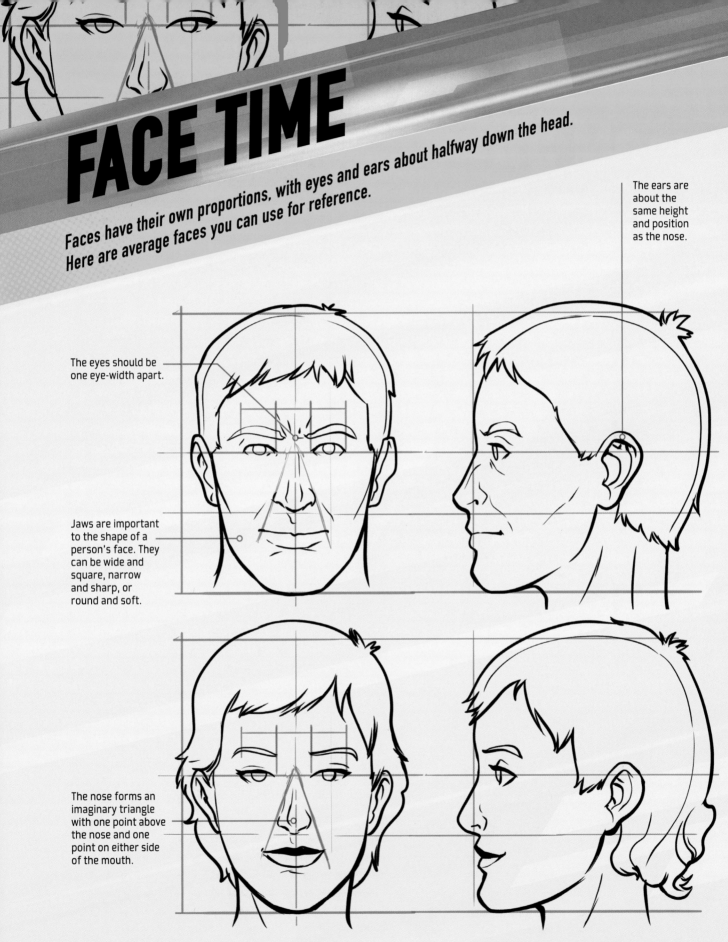

Look at your friends' and family members' faces. You will see many variations. Sketch the details you see and study their hairstyles. You can use traits like these to make each of your comic characters unique.

FROM START TO FINISH

If you're brimming with ideas, you can jump straight into drawing your comic book. For most creators, a good page of comic art requires a bit of preparation.

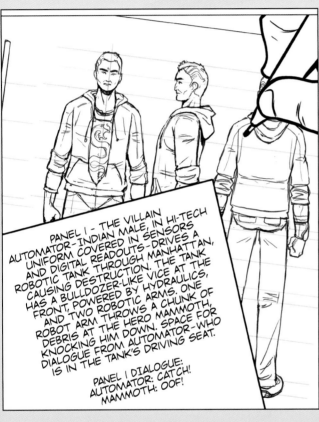

PANEL 1 - THE VILLAIN AUTOMATOR - INDIAN MALE, IN HI-TECH UNIFORM COVERED IN SENSORS AND DIGITAL READOUTS - DRIVES A ROBOTIC TANK THROUGH MANHATTAN, CAUSING DESTRUCTION. THE TANK HAS A BULLDOZER-LIKE VICE AT THE FRONT, POWERED BY HYDRAULICS, AND TWO ROBOTIC ARMS. ONE ROBOT ARM THROWS A CHUNK OF DEBRIS AT THE HERO MAMMOTH, KNOCKING HIM DOWN. SPACE FOR DIALOGUE FROM AUTOMATOR-WHO IS IN THE TANK'S DRIVING SEAT.

PANEL 1 DIALOGUE:
AUTOMATOR: CATCH!
MAMMOTH: OOF!

1. THE SCRIPT

First, plan your story. Think about the characters who appear in the adventure. What do they look like, what do they wear, and how do they behave? Then, write your story with notes on the action that will take place on each page.

2. THUMBNAILS

Now you can map out a page. These first small, rough sketches for page layouts are called **THUMBNAILS**. When you're happy with the layout, you can move to a larger sheet of paper and prepare for the finished artwork.

3. THE PANELS

Draw the panels lightly on the page and mark where the **SPEECH BALLOONS** will go. Then you can start drawing details in pencil, starting wherever you like on the page.

4. PERSPECTIVE

Guidelines for **PERSPECTIVE** help create a 3D environment for many scenes. You can start drawing your characters as stick figures so that you get their poses and positions right.

5. DIALOGUE

Draw the final details in pencil. Add ruled lines to the speech balloons and write the dialogue between them.

6. COLORING IN

Go over the pencil sketches in ink with a pen or brush, including the panels and speech balloons. Once the ink is dry, you can erase the pencil lines. Finally, it's time for the colors!

SPACE SQUADRON

Originating from different worlds, our four galactic heroes are very different in personality, shape, and style. Here are some pointers to use when creating your own comic characters.

TAKING CHARGE

When creating a leader for a team, don't always go for the obvious choice. Captor is the strongest warrior in the Outriders, but he is a loner. Star Runner is a tough, experienced soldier and by far the best strategist, who will look out for all her teammates.

NAME: STAR RUNNER

REAL IDENTITY: Glory Keyes

POWERS: Space pilot and engineer.

ORIGIN: After disobeying orders to save her team, Captain Keyes was drummed out of the Space Corps and formed her own platoon for hire.

STRENGTH ◆◆◇◇◇
INTELLIGENCE ◆◆◆◆◇
SPECIAL POWERS ◆◆◇◇◇
FIGHTING SKILLS ◆◆◆◇◇

ENVIRO-SUIT

Consider your characters' needs in outer space. As a human, Star Runner needs a spacesuit to survive the rigors of cold, airless space. Her suit is based on an early twenty-first-century design but is leaner due to advances in space wear since interstellar travel became possible.

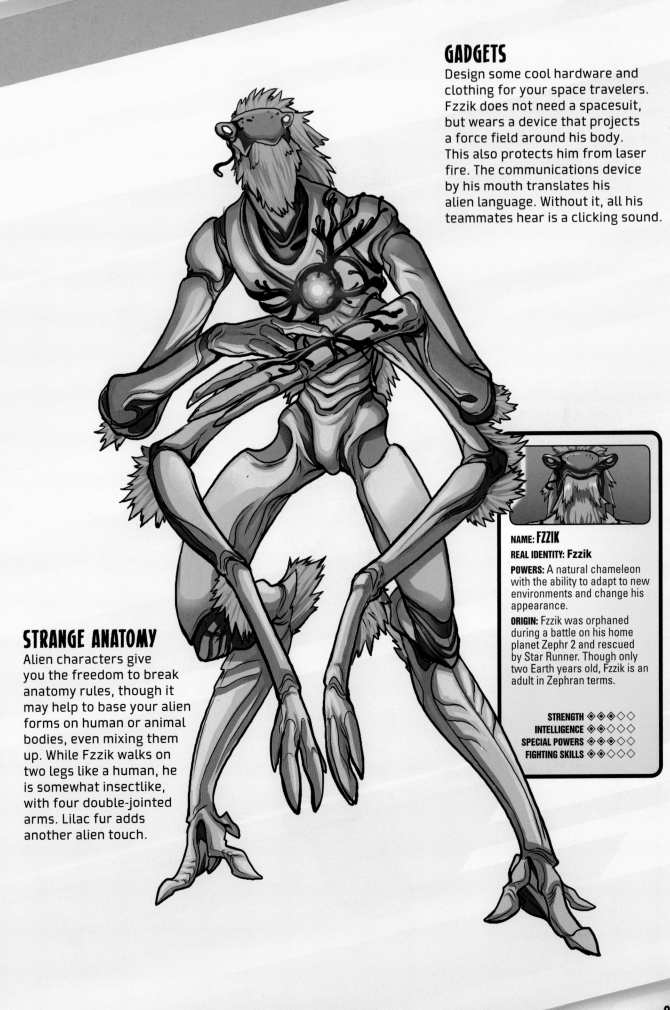

GADGETS

Design some cool hardware and clothing for your space travelers. Fzzik does not need a spacesuit, but wears a device that projects a force field around his body. This also protects him from laser fire. The communications device by his mouth translates his alien language. Without it, all his teammates hear is a clicking sound.

STRANGE ANATOMY

Alien characters give you the freedom to break anatomy rules, though it may help to base your alien forms on human or animal bodies, even mixing them up. While Fzzik walks on two legs like a human, he is somewhat insectlike, with four double-jointed arms. Lilac fur adds another alien touch.

NAME: FZZIK

REAL IDENTITY: Fzzik

POWERS: A natural chameleon with the ability to adapt to new environments and change his appearance.

ORIGIN: Fzzik was orphaned during a battle on his home planet Zephr 2 and rescued by Star Runner. Though only two Earth years old, Fzzik is an adult in Zephran terms.

STRENGTH ◆◆◆◇◇
INTELLIGENCE ◆◆◇◇◇
SPECIAL POWERS ◆◆◆◆◇
FIGHTING SKILLS ◆◆◇◇◇

GEAR CHANGE

Robot bodies are built up from simple **GEOMETRIC** shapes. Proto has a basic human form but with metal parts. Whoever designed him loved the old tech of cogs, rods, and gears, but new pirate tech has been added to his systems to make this math android more useful in battle. The two technologies are contrasting.

NAME: PROTO

REAL IDENTITY: Pro-T-O

POWERS: Familiar with all types of alien tech and weapons; fires laser beams from eyes; excellent accountancy skills.

ORIGIN: This mathematical android designed by Sol Stocks Inc. was stolen during a heist, and upgraded and reprogrammed by pirates.

STRENGTH	◆◆◆◆◇
INTELLIGENCE	◆◆◆◆◆
SPECIAL POWERS	◆◆◆◆◇
FIGHTING SKILLS	◆◆◆◆◇

PURPOSE BUILT

When building machinery, including robots, think about the purpose of each part. The cables along Proto's limbs are **HYDRAULIC** and give him movement. He is powered by solar energy cells on his shoulders. The cogs inside his chest are his central processing unit or brain.

RELOCATION

What cultures do your alien characters come from? Captor is a galactic tough-guy whose red-colored skin reflects his fiery heritage. He has a wild attitude and a background similar to that of Earth's Viking warriors. Imagine how other societies from Earth's past might develop in a new or hostile environment on another planet. How would they be different?

NAME: CAPTOR

REAL IDENTITY: Grail Tor

POWERS: Fierce fighter, excellent tracker.

ORIGIN: Galactic bounty hunter Tor was framed for treason he didn't commit. Adopting a new identity as Captor, he now hunts space criminals as part of the Outriders.

STRENGTH	◇◇◇◇◇
INTELLIGENCE	◇◇◇◇◇
SPECIAL POWERS	◇◇◇◇◇
FIGHTING SKILLS	◇◇◇◇◇

NEW WORLDS, NEW WEAPONS

This alien warrior wears armor and carries various exotic weapons. While he is happy to use advanced blaster weapons, the blades he carries suggest he prefers hand-to-hand combat. Try to give your cosmic characters clothes and weapons with an alien twist. Invent new fashions and weapons for new aliens who have never visited Earth.

STELLAR GUARD

The cloned peacekeeper Star Sentinel patrols our galaxy, guided by his robot companion, Valis. Bring him to life, so that he can use his stellar scepter to prevent interplanetary war.

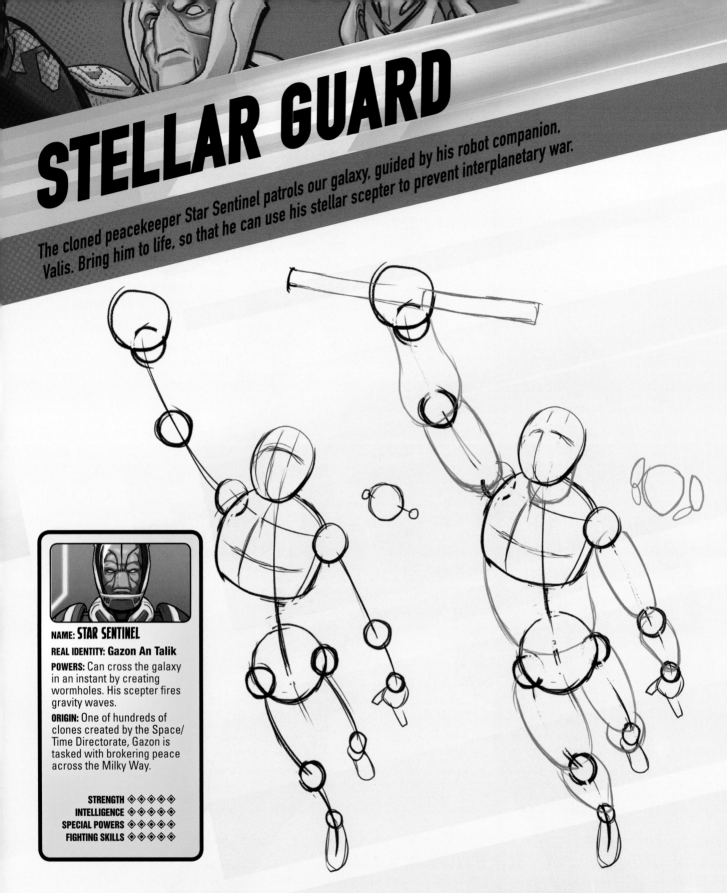

NAME: STAR SENTINEL

REAL IDENTITY: Gazon An Talik

POWERS: Can cross the galaxy in an instant by creating wormholes. His scepter fires gravity waves.

ORIGIN: One of hundreds of clones created by the Space/Time Directorate, Gazon is tasked with brokering peace across the Milky Way.

STRENGTH ◆◆◆◆◆◆
INTELLIGENCE ◆◆◆◆◆
SPECIAL POWERS ◆◆◆◆◆
FIGHTING SKILLS ◆◆◆◆◆

1. WIRE FRAME

Draw a simple, jointed stick figure to show the pose of your hero soaring through space. His right hand holds his scepter of power and reaches toward the reader. Indicate his robot companion with a circle.

2. BLOCK FIGURE

Bulk out Star Sentinel's body with 3D shapes. As the scepter pulls him toward you, his left hand appears to be about as large as his head, and his body gets thinner toward his toes. This effect is called **FORESHORTENING**.

3. ANATOMY

Star Sentinel has an alien face but similar anatomy to a human. Start giving definition to his muscles. Note that his head is pushed back as he looks forward, while his lower body is turned at a slight angle.

4. FINISHED PENCIL SKETCHES

You can now add the details of the protective space uniform over Star Sentinel's body, including his jacket, belt, padding, and clear helmet. Draw the grid pattern on his costume last, curving the lines around his body.

COMPUTER COMPANION

I'M GETTING REPORTS OF **BORDER INCURSIONS** ON POPL-5.

Star Sentinel has a robot companion, Valis, to give him reports, directions, and to open miniature wormholes to transport the pair of them across the galaxy in an instant.

Having another character to talk to helps when it comes to writing a story for the hero. Valis can give Star Sentinel instructions and even make jokes with the hero. Without Valis, Star Sentinel will have to talk to himself... or it will be a very quiet comic!

5. INKS
Carefully ink the lines you want to keep, using a brush or pen. You may want to use a fine-line pen to draw the grid and patterns on his uniform, to keep the lines a regular thickness, and to complete any technical details on the scepter and robot.

6. COLORS
Star Sentinel wears a uniform rather than a superhero costume. It looks more official than a soldier's uniform. He is permitted to use force if peace negotiations fail. The colors and style of his suit match the design of his robot.

TOP TIP
Star Sentinel wears a mix of uniform and spacesuit. Try adding space tech or body armor to regular clothes for your own cosmic characters' clothing.

INSPIRED ALIENS

Meet the locals! If you need inspiration for how to fill the galaxy with amazing alien creatures, just look at the strange animals that live on Earth.

NAME: GRANIX DUR

REAL IDENTITY: Granix Dur

POWERS: Sharpshooting bounty hunter with an armored hide.

ORIGIN: A former bandit from the planet Termund, Granix Dur left home in search of greater gains.

STRENGTH ◆◆◆◆◇
INTELLIGENCE ◆◆◇◇◇
SPECIAL POWERS ◆◆◇◇◇
FIGHTING SKILLS ◆◆◆◆◇

▲ The giant armadillo is a South American mammal with flexible armored plating and long claws used for tearing through the earth for food.

➤ Imagine the armadillo walking on hind legs, with a **BANDOLIER** across his chest and a warp blaster in his claw.

NAME: SKRIIL

REAL IDENTITY: Skriil

POWERS: This high-jumping insectoid serves overpriced fast food and juicy rumors.

ORIGIN: Skriil dreamed of joining his 427 brothers in the airborne Locust Legion, but after a failed medical exam, he could only get work as a chef on the galaxy's outer rim.

STRENGTH ◆◇◇◇◇
INTELLIGENCE ◆◆◇◇◇
SPECIAL POWERS ◆◇◇◇◇
FIGHTING SKILLS ◆◇◇◇◇

▲ The grasshopper is a vegetarian insect, with powerful back legs used for leaping between plants to escape danger.

➤ Enlarge the grasshopper to human size and give it thorny arms and legs; now it looks quite intimidating, even in a restaurant uniform!

The angle parentheses < > around the aliens' words mean that the dialogue is a translation from their language.

Dressed in clothing, the giant insect appears intelligent. It looks menacing but fragile.

Give the creature green skin, and it's an instant extraterrestrial! The bandoliers and armor suggest it's a survivor from an outlaw planet—not a creature you want to mess with!

TOP TIP
Don't be afraid of mixing and matching Earth creatures to design new aliens. How about crab claws on an ape or tentacles on a spider?

ROBOT RENDERING

Robots are commonplace in the worlds at the edges of our galaxy. Here are the nuts and bolts of constructing your own range of mechanical wonders.

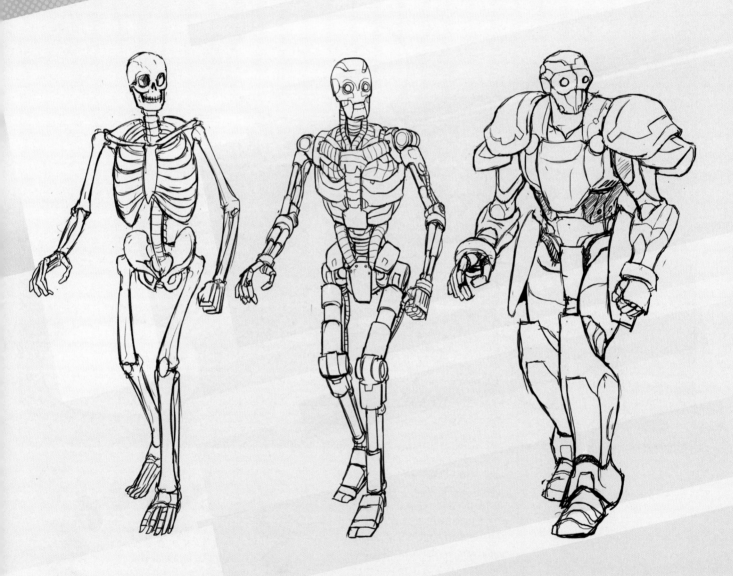

1. Androids are robots designed to mimic humans. This one is designed to be a service android, built for indoor tasks, not fighting. To construct it, first sketch a human skeleton.

2. Gradually replace the bones with mechanical parts. Where the mechanical pieces meet, draw rivets and screws. Exaggerate body parts—expand the chest, while keeping the lower torso thin.

3. If you want your robot to be ready for action, cover some parts of the frame with molded metal plates. Add a power pack and light-up eyes to help your android function during day and night.

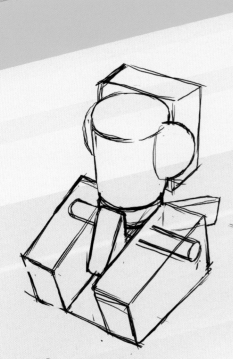 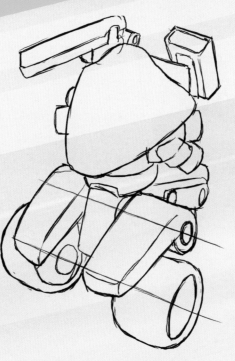 

1. Robots can be any size or shape. This one runs on wheels and is built around a series of 3D shapes. It is a war robot, designed to be tough and deliver massive firepower.

2. More parts are added, and 3D shapes are given smoother outlines. The chunky tires are designed for crossing extreme terrain. The machine has a sleek laser cannon mounted on one shoulder.

3. Lines are added to the bodywork to show how the frame is assembled. Vents have been added to the hood, and joints are placed between sections to show how the war robot can turn and raise weapons.

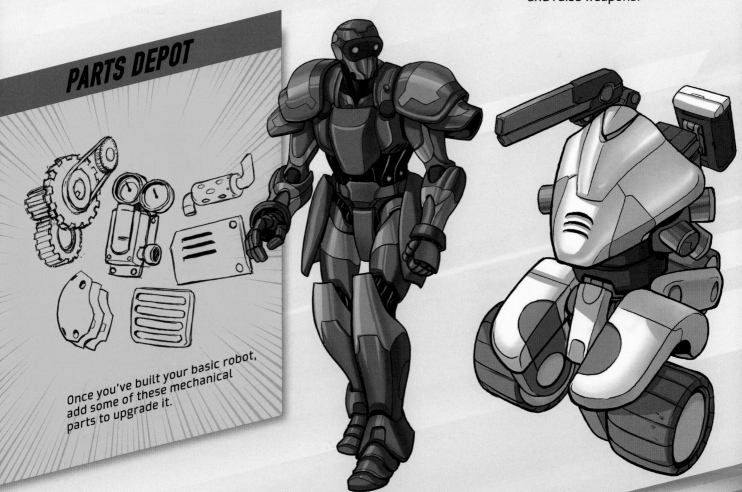

PARTS DEPOT

Once you've built your basic robot, add some of these mechanical parts to upgrade it.

LAUNCH BAY

Your cosmic heroes are going to need some transportation to get around. Here's how to design your own concept speedsters and spaceships, starting with real-life objects or simple shapes.

The BroncoTEC is a two-person hovering speedster used for jetting around the badlands of the planet Rachma, dodging mech rustlers. The design is based around a motorcycle chopper, with wings replacing wheels. Dust and grime on the vehicle show it is used in a hostile environment.

Consider how your alien vehicle is powered and what propulsion system it uses. The BroncoTEC is solar-powered and speeds along using rear jets and hover fans under the wings.

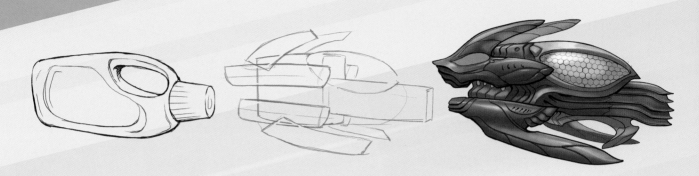

Inspiration for transportation can come from anywhere, not just existing vehicles. This Vespid fighter is based on a household detergent bottle! The cap has been extended to create a nose cone. The pilot sits inside the handle, and jagged fins sprout from the rear, surrounding its nuclear propulsion engine.

This Vespid is one of a squadron of fighters that are part of the United System of Gwalor's planetary defense corps. The cockpit has space for just one fighter pilot. The ship is armed with extending plasma cannons—one on each side—with two radon torpedoes ready for launch from the nose cone.

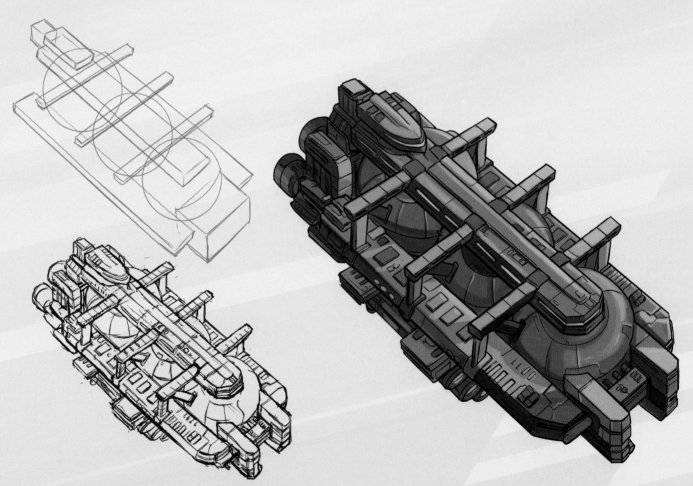

This space freighter doesn't have to have an aerodynamic shape. It is designed for long voyages and carrying large cargo—mainly metrinium from the mines of Kalso. It is built around a collection of 3D shapes—three large spheres for cargo—held together by a frame where the crew live and work.

There is nothing glamorous about this transportation vehicle. The bodywork is made up of thousands of metal plates. The windows and lights look tiny, which tells you how massive it is. It is too big to land on a planet. The crew leaves it in orbit and uses shuttles to visit other worlds.

GALAXY GUIDE

With a whole universe to explore, your characters will discover alien worlds very different than our own, full of exotic plants and animals, plus unique and often hostile environments.

TOP TIP

Create a challenge for your cosmic heroes by sending them to worlds with high gravity, poisonous air, no sun, or extreme weather.

NAME: VRADEX

POWERS: Batlike aliens that can survive intense cold and find their way in the dark using sonar.

ORIGIN: Since the Ryassan Corporation began deep drilling on their planet, the Vradex's sonar has been affected. They are fighting to force the Ryassans out.

STRENGTH ◆◇◇◇◇
INTELLIGENCE ◆◇◇◇◇
SPECIAL POWERS ◆◆◇◇◇
FIGHTING SKILLS ◆◆◇◇◇

JUNGLE WAR

The Vradex are at war with the Ryassans. On the Vradex planet, the Ryassan troops need to wear enviro-suits. The soldiers are easy pickings for the Vradex warriors, who are used to these cold and shadowy conditions.

When you're inventing a planet, think about its position in space. Far away from a sun, the Vradex world is dark, with tangles of black vinelike plants that receive little light. The plants are watered by a creeping fog.

SCORCHED WORLD

Earth has many different environments that may inspire your alien worlds—jungles, mountains, tundra, oceans, and deserts. By changing colors and including new plants and animals, you can transform a landscape.

Populate the sky with new moons, bizarre flying creatures, and futuristic airships, and a desert world becomes much stranger than any landscape on Earth. With the sun so large in the sky, this planet is extremely hot and dry. The locals have to look far and dig deep to find water.

STAR FIELD

In reality, the vacuum of space is largely empty. For a dramatic space setting, add rocky asteroids and gaseous clouds in the black void.

To add random groups of stars to your background, dip an old toothbrush in white paint, and then flick your finger over the bristles to spray white specks over the black areas. Be sure to do this before you add characters!

PLANET IN PERIL

Let's create a dramatic action scene set on an alien planet. The Absorbots are threatening to sap the life energy of the lush planet Phylla. Help the Outriders and Star Sentinel protect this world from annihilation.

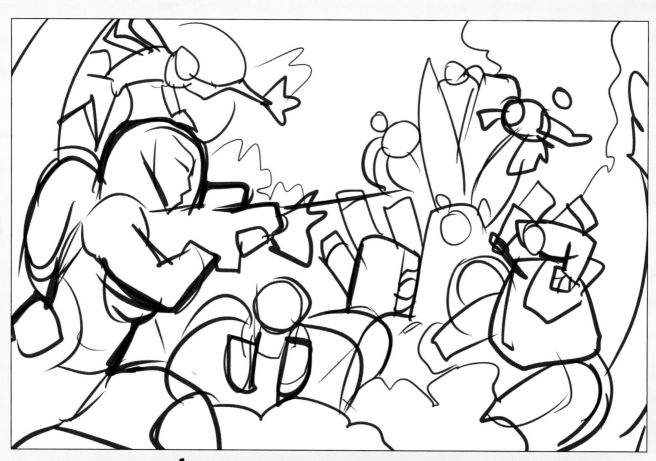

1. Roughly plan the position of your heroes and robotic villains in the alien scene. The Absorbots are defending their life-draining machine from attack. This is where the action is directed.

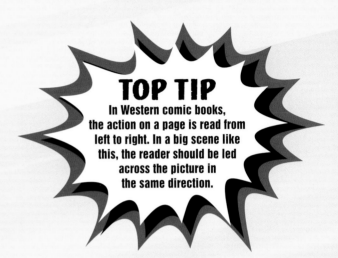

TOP TIP
In Western comic books, the action on a page is read from left to right. In a big scene like this, the reader should be led across the picture in the same direction.

2. Build up the figures and machinery with 3D shapes. The grid of perspective lines shows the direction of the action, starting with Star Runner on the left, and moving toward the Absorbots' machine, on the right.

TOP TIP

Avoid placing all your characters in the same range, as it can make a scene feel flat. This picture works well because it has a lot of depth, with heroes up close and in the distance.

3. In these sketches, the curves of the plant life contrast with the blocky shapes of the Absorbots. The alien plants resemble an Earth coral reef, but they are growing above ground.

NAME: ABSORBOTS

POWERS: Mechanical creatures that use animal and plant life as their power source.

ORIGIN: A cybernetic experiment gone wrong, the Absorbots learned to duplicate themselves, but can't produce their own power. They threaten all carbon-based life.

STRENGTH ◆◆◆◆◇
INTELLIGENCE ◆◆◆◇◇
SPECIAL POWERS ◆◆◆◆◇
FIGHTING SKILLS ◆◆◇◇◇

4. The finished scene is inked. Bolder outlines help the characters stand out from the background. There is a lot going on, but your eye should be led around the scene quite easily.

DEFENSE FORCE

The finished battle scene is lit up with laser and plasma fire. The plant life on Phylla is blue, while the atmosphere is green, giving the scene a cool and unnatural tint that suits the otherworldly setting.

KEEP IT SNAPPY!

Can you make comic dialogue lively and fun? Different worlds and different cultures mean different opinions. Keep your comic characters distinct by giving them diverse personalities — and add a little humor!

Not everyone talks the same. When you develop a new character, whether human or alien, give some thought to how they react to the world and other characters. Are they bossy, considerate, angry, or always cracking jokes?

> I'M SURE I'VE SEEN YOUR REVOLTING FACE ON A WANTED POSTER ...
>
> GIVE ME ONE GOOD REASON WHY I SHOULDN'T SHOOT YOU DEAD AND CLAIM THE REWARD!
>
> WELL, STRICTLY SPEAKING, SIR, AS AN ANDROID, I'VE NEVER BEEN ALIVE, SO I WOULD JUST BE TEMPORARILY OUT OF SERVICE.

It may help to imagine your hero or villain acting or talking like a character you've seen in a movie or cartoon. Then you can imagine their voice in your head, talking in a distinct way. Here, Star Sentinel is heroic but innocent, while his robot Valis talks like a slightly patronizing adult.

> MY SCEPTER IS FAILING ME! I'M BEING SUCKED TOWARD THE BLACK HOLE!
>
> HAVE YOU TRIED SWITCHING IT OFF AND ON AGAIN?

In outer-space adventures, your characters are going to encounter lots of alien cultures and technologies they don't understand. These encounters can lead to nail-biting or humorous scenes.

> I CAN'T GET USED TO THE WAY YOU DRINK THROUGH YOUR NOSE!
>
> NOSE?! THIS ISN'T MY NOSE!

GLOSSARY

BANDOLIER A shoulder belt with loops or pockets for ammunition.

FORESHORTENING A perspective effect that makes objects appear closer.

GEOMETRIC Made up of regular lines and shapes, for example, a pattern made of squares, triangles, or circles.

HYDRAULIC Moved using water under pressure.

PERSPECTIVE A way of representing three-dimensional (3D) objects in a picture.

SPEECH BALLOON A shape used in comic panels to hold character dialogue.

THUMBNAIL A rough small-scale sketch used for planning a page layout.

TORSO The upper part of the human body, without the head, neck, arms, or legs.

FURTHER INFORMATION

Books to read

Drawing Manga: Step by Step by Ben Krefta (Arcturus Publishing, 2013)

How to Draw 101 Space Aliens by Barry Green (Top That Publishing, 2014)

How to Draw Incredible Aliens and Cool Space Stuff by Fiona Gowen (Barron's Educational Series, 2015)

Stan Lee's How to Draw Superheroes by Stan Lee (Watson-Guptill, 2013)

Star Wars Drawing Manual by Lucasfilm (Egmont, 2016)

Write and Draw Your Own Comics by Louise Stowell and Jess Bradley (Usborne, 2014)

Websites

PowerKids Press has developed an online list of websites related to the subject of this book. This site is updated regularly. Please use this link to access the list:
www.powerkidslinks.com/uca/cosmic

INDEX

Published in 2018 by **The Rosen Publishing Group, Inc.**
29 East 21st Street, New York, NY 10010

CATALOGING-IN-PUBLICATION DATA

Names: Potter, William.
Title: Drawing cosmic heroes / William Potter and Juan Calle.
Description: New York : PowerKids Press, 2018. | Series: Ultimate comic art | Includes index.
Identifiers: ISBN 9781508154716 (pbk.) | ISBN 9781508154655 (library bound) | ISBN 9781508154532 (6 pack)
Subjects: LCSH: Science fiction comic books, strips, etc.--Technique--Juvenile literature. | Heroes in art--Juvenile literature. | Figure drawing--Technique--Juvenile literature. | Comic books, strips, etc.--Technique--Juvenile literature.
Classification: LCC NC1764.8.S35 P68 2018 | DDC 741.5'1--dc23

Copyright © 2018 Arcturus Holdings Limited

Text: William Potter
Illustrations: Juan Calle and Info Liberum
Design: Neal Cobourne
Design series edition: Emma Randall
Editor: Joe Harris

Manufactured in the United States of America
CPSIA Compliance Information: Batch BS17PK: For Further Information contact Rosen Publishing, New York, New York at 1-800-237-9932.